N

DETERMINATION, PERSEVERANCE, ATTITUDE

Norm
Determination, Perseverance, Attitude
All Rights Reserved.
Copyright © 2019 Norm Roberge
v2.0

The opinions expressed in this manuscript are solely the opinions of the author and do not represent the opinions or thoughts of the publisher. The author has represented and warranted full ownership and/or legal right to publish all the materials in this book.

This book may not be reproduced, transmitted, or stored in whole or in part by any means, including graphic, electronic, or mechanical without the express written consent of the publisher except in the case of brief quotations embodied in critical articles and reviews.

Outskirts Press, Inc.
http://www.outskirtspress.com

ISBN: 978-1-9772-0463-9

Cover Photo © 2019 www.gettyimages.com. All rights reserved - used with permission.

Outskirts Press and the "OP" logo are trademarks belonging to Outskirts Press, Inc.

PRINTED IN THE UNITED STATES OF AMERICA

Table of Contents

Introduction		i
1	Norm	1
2	The Anguish, The Fear, The Reality, The Sadness	7
3	The Long Road Home	13
4	Determination, Perseverance and Attitude	21
5	Keep on Keeping On – The Challenges The Rewards	26
6	ADA – Ahead of the Time	31
7	Technology to the Rescue	37
8	Another Change Improvements for Hunting and Other Challenges	41
9	Day Camp	50

10	October Hunting Season My Favorite Time of Year	53
11	Jasper of Hillside not a Service Dog but a Hunting Buddy	66
12	Beginning New Challenges	69
13	The Stretch	76
14	Back Home – Now What?	92
15	Sadness With Very Fond Memories	108
16	Devastating	110
Why Did I Write This Book?		122
Epilogue		123

Introduction
By Jessica Couto (Norm's Daughter)

I'm not sure I remember that horrific day, or I relive it through other's telling the story so many times. I recall heading to McDonald's with my mother, brother and a family friend. On our way there, we saw an ambulance heading in the opposite direction. My mother, a nurse, said, "Hmm that ambulance is driving slowly, it must be a spinal cord injury." Seconds later she saw my father's friend Jay's truck following behind the ambulance and realized that something was wrong. We immediately turned around and headed to the hospital. I stayed in the car with my 2-year-old brother trying to entertain him. Little did we know our life was about to change.

Change…doesn't always have to be a bad thing. I remember him coming home from rehabilitation and squeezing him so hard, that I heard him tell his friend Scott, "Ohh that kind of hurt my neck." I was ecstatic that my dad was ALIVE and HOME! Since I was only 6 when my father became paralyzed, I don't remember life before his accident. My normal has always been my dad in a wheelchair and my parents did the best at giving my brother and me a NORMAL childhood.

I remember our first trip to Disney World, which was not long after my father's accident. My grandfather was pushing my dad's wheelchair around the park. My dad was getting mad at him, because he wanted to do it himself. Others would have said, "Oh Norm is so stubborn," but in reality, that was my Dad saying to others, "I don't want to rely on you, I've got this!" From that point on, my dad was independent and never let his disability stop him. Every summer we would go camping at Old Orchard Beach. It was amazing to see my dad transfer himself from the wheelchair to the pop-up camper. People would stare at him, and I would think "YUP< that's my dad, isn't he COOL." He was my hero… he never let his disability get him down. And if he did, he never showed it to my brother or me. I'm sure my mom knew, and I know things were tougher on her, as she had to pick up where he couldn't.

Don't get me wrong, there was things I did miss out on, but we always tried to find a way to partake, it would just be different. My senior year of high school, my dad was in the hospital. My friends and I were all dressed up, so we went to visit him to get a picture with him. My wedding day, he still walked me down the aisle with my mom on one side and him on the other. My mom and I were only worried he would run over the dress… well because there were the things that he wouldn't mean to do, but they would always happen. Sure I wasn't able to dance with him at my wedding, but I was able to honor him and my mom with a video of all our memories together. We had the blessing of being able to graduate college together. I was known as "Norm's Daughter at the University. Those that know him, wouldn't be surprised that he was known throughout the school. My kids laugh now when we go to visit them, they say, "Grampy" talks to everyone, and everyone knows him."

Five years ago, I was diagnosed with breast cancer, and had to undergo a double mastectomy, chemotherapy and radiation, treatment that lasted 2 years. I approached it all with a positive attitude and made light of the situations I was in. I truly believe that came from all the things I learned from watching my dad. He could have gone down a different path when he got in his accident, but he chose the right one. Sometimes he forgets he's in a wheelchair and doesn't make the smartest choices. Like the time he dropped my mom off at the airport for her to fly to Florida to visit me. He decided he was going to ride the escalator with his wheelchair. YES... THAT'S MY DAD!!

Chapter 1

Norm

IT WAS JULY, in Berlin NH and the hottest week that summer. Wednesday night after we put the kids to bed, my wife Jeanne and I decided to watch a movie. My attitude was not the best and I decided that I would call in sick the next day because my boss had really pissed me off.

The following morning my 2 kids were playing in the yard and I was on "kid duty" because my wife was at work and we didn't need the sitter as I was home. Lunch and a water hose cool off followed. A quick phone call to my buddy Jay about dirt bike riding and a follow up call to the babysitter Lucille. A plan is in place. Jay arrives we load up the dirt bike, let Lucille know we will be gone for a couple of hours and head for the sand pit in Gorham. Bikes unloaded check, oil gas riding gear on "ready ride". Jay puts his keys in the truck turns to see where I was.

He couldn't see me or hear the noise from my exhaust pipe. Where the hell did Norm go?

My life was rich with family, grandfather, aunts, and uncles. My father's sister married my mother's brother four generations, both grandparents bought campers at Akers Pond and lots of opportunity for fun at camp during the summer. At five I lived on Cambridge Street in a little house between two apartment buildings, kids everywhere. As a curious kid will do I wanted to see what was in the cellar so headed down the stairs to check it out. Took the first step, missed the second step and fell down twelve stairs. Hospital here I come. Broken collar bone. Not too many years later while at camp I decided to make a fire, my brother Leo had put gas in the kerosene can, unbeknown to me and whoops I took the can, spread it over the wood in the fireplace then dropped a steel plate over the top to keep the flame in the fireplace. When I lit a match flames came straight out into my face burning my eyebrows and hair.

I attended St Regis Catholic School. If you had an older brother attending the school you didn't stand a chance with getting away with anything. A science fair award demonstrating how much water can the sun pull form the earth? I took third prize and my friend Ramsey took second demonstrating what would happen if a meteorite hit the Earth. High School was crazy 1500 students. My brother Leo and Don kept our parents busy, I was the quiet guy. We had developed a "gang/click" girls included were all part of it helping us build gas operated go carts, from punch buggies that we bought for $100. Fix them up ride around until the fenders would fall off or the cops would take us off the road. Once I took a 650 BSA motor cycle and turned it into a 3-wheeler, police department did not think too much of that either. Back in the day Berlin NH was a booming City of 35,000 people, the paper mill was a great employment opportunity this is where my Dad worked, and Mom worked at converse Sneaker Factory. We never had to worry about what we were wearing on our feet. In 12th grade

I found my true love, Jeanne. We shared several classes together and she was hot!

Big brother's set up little brother with a date. Next thing you know big brother marries Jeanne's sister Denise and I marry Jeanne. My poor mother in law stuck with two Roberge's. 24 years old and two kids Jessica and Nathan. Cute kids if I say so myself.

Life is good I join the National Guard for extra money this was a great environment for me. It gave me extra money for the family and it was a rockum sockum opportunity. I was never the person to sit back while some smart ass starts kicking me around. I loved the physical stamina that the National Guard demanded. Running 5 miles 7 days a week, push-ups ladder bar, sit ups with a time limit. Duck hunting was my second love. I would average 100 ducks and 15 geese a season. I was very lucky that Jeanne would put up with my obsession with hunting. A trip to Three Rivers, Quebec and camping out on an island for two nights. We had reports that the island was a good place for duck hunters. The first morning was crazy we woke up with water in our tent, our sleeping bags were wet, there was so many ducks flying I said the hell with my sleeping bag I loaded my gun and started shooting ducks in my underwear. My buddy Cricket thought the island was sinking at first then he noticed his beer was floating away. I shot 5 ducks while Cricket saved his beer. We had a great time.

Cricket and I made a bet that I would beat him in the 5-mile PUB race in Berlin. We were both training, but the race never happened.

When I drove over the top of the bank on my dirt bike on the hot July afternoon, as I started to go down the bank it wasn't there. The front tire just dropped straight down throwing me off the bike and freefall to the bottom of the pit, landing on my face. Jay is standing at the top of the bank looking down and sees my laying on my back. As I lay there not able to move, my body felt like it fell asleep, but I couldn't shake off the tingling feeling. I could see the clouds racing by and I saw Jay looking down to see if I was ok. The prickling feeling was getting worse. I tried moving any parts of my body, but nothing was moving? My first thought was, shit I broke my neck, just like the guy in the movie

Jeanne and I watched last night. The guy in the movie dives into the ocean and breaks his neck. When I left the house, I told Lucille, the baby sitter, where we were going riding, because I always joked with Lucille on the way out I said to her, "if I'm not home by six o'clock I broke my neck. This was supposed to be a joke.

Here I am lying in a sandpit barely breathing, body burning inside clouds racing I'm thinking "I'm going to die alone and in a sandpit. MY wife and kids what are they going to do? I'm not a church going person but I was praying then. Jay gets back with the ambulance and after they moved me from the ground to the ambulance there were these sharp jagged rocks that I was laying on, I never felt them. It was only 7 miles away, but it was the slowest ride from Gorham to the Berlin hospital in the ambulance.

Chapter 2

THE ANGUISH, THE FEAR, THE REALITY, THE SADNESS

As the ambulance headed to the Hospital in Berlin, my wife Jeanne was driving to Gorham with the kids and the babysitter heading to McDonalds. She saw the ambulance lights flashing and our friend Jay's car driving slowly behind the ambulance, but without me. Two bikes in the back of the truck but I was not on the passenger side.

At last the ambulance arrives at the emergency room, I am rushed to the x-ray for pictures of my neck. It took a little time, but my family arrived at the hospital. While this was happening my wife, who worked at St Luke's Medical Center at the time, all the doctors were our friends, they wanted to help. I'm in x-ray looking at the ceiling thinking about the guy who broke his neck in the movie we watched the night before. Thought of all the care I was going to need, I laid there and cried inside.

Finally, the x-rays came back I severed my C-6 and C-07 bones in my neck. In other words, I'm paralyzed from the neck down. The nurse then told me that they cut off my leather pants. I was wild!! I really like them. They were awesome. That's when I began to realize I'm in trouble. This is real I didn't feel them cutting my leather pants off.

I could hear the doctors telling my wife Jeanne. "This isn't good. We need to get him to Hanover, NH Dartmouth Medical Center. It took us 5 ½ hours to get there, on the way we were stopped by the state troopers for traveling too slow. In the meantime, my brain was going crazy with thoughts of my kid's future, like who was going to teach them ways of life that I could not do as a "normal Dad. My relationship with Jeanne, where is that going to go with me being incapable of making love to her. I was so wrong with that thought, my love for Jeanne grows every day. Without her on my side I would not be where I am today. Love comes from your heart not your penis.

The emergency crew at Hanover was ready they rushed me to the x-ray room for more pictures of my injury. I came out looking like a hot dog between a bun. The surgeons had these 7-inch bars with holes at each end then took 2 ¼ inch screws and drilled a hole on each side of my head and screwed a metal bar on each side of my head, with a five-pound sand bag tied to them. Ouch!!! I'm paralyzed but I do have feeling on my head!

Here I am strapped between tow frames and a five-pound bag tied to the metal bars screwed into my head. The nurses would come in every 4 hours and rotate my position, 4 hours starting at the ceiling and 4 hours of staring at the floor. Now it's time to eat, it took several days to adjust to eating lying face down. It sucked! Two days of being flipped like a hot dog on a grill. This became the moment of acceptance. I consciously decided to accept what happened, it was time to move on. I was still sad, and I still cried inside but I recognized I had to work hard. I worked very hard at eating on my belly. Visitors' would lay down underneath my frame and talk to me. I don't know how I did it but I began to fantasize this could be a new adventure and a big challenge for my family. Little did I realize at this moment, what that really meant. At this point what it did mean for me, was if I'm positive about my new life and people see that, they will get comfortable being around me and hopefully they leave my room with a good feeling about my future. This was just a thought – but a good one. Positive thinking at a very critical time.

New reality it was time to have a team meeting regarding my condition and future needs, and it all sounded bad. The doctors said that I was paralyzed from the neck down! I kept looking at Jeanne and thinking our life is going to be a living hell. At this time, we were living in a rented apartment on the second floor. We had a good size yard and woods behind the house, 2 kids and a wife who was happy. That changed fast.

I didn't sleep much that night and many more thinking my life was over as a normal person. My ability to help with taking care of my children as they grow up, like baseball, basketball, dancing, swimming, nature walks and all those things you take for granted. How will I support my family? Who is going to hire a guy in a wheelchair? How will Jeanne handle all this pressure for the rest of her life? Being a nurse Jeanne knew how much work this was going to be for her. The devil of depression found its' way through my intended positive thinking. Reality, my life was going to suck for me, Jeanne, and the kids. Accepting, this new reality, was not going well. Dreams of walking around the mill and no one saying, "where is your wheelchair"? Dreams about little green men from New Hampshire give me crap about not being able to walk. Sleepless nights and nightmares. Thank God for Betty and Jim. I had the greatest nurse you could ever have. Her name was Betty, I wanted her to come with us! She gave me the courage to look beyond my disability and go forward. Don't bother looking back, what is done is done! There was a male nurse who worked the night shift and he would sit on the floor and look up at me and talk for hours until I fell asleep. He would bring in a six pack of diet Pepsi and share it with me during the week.

Physical therapy started with sitting in the chair without falling out. I had no balance it wasn't easy. My first thoughts were, this sucks. But I had to make another commitment that I was going to keep a positive attitude. I had two wonderful kids and a wife who was worth living for. As I worked harder and harder at therapy there was a lot of pain where the screws were into the side of my head, every time I did an exercise it would hurt. They offered me pain pills, but I refused, I needed to learn to live with pain. Hanover was done with what they could do for me now it was up to me. It was time to move on to a rehab center at Woburn Mass. The quicker I got there, the quicker I get home, yeah!

Chapter 3

THE LONG ROAD HOME

Two hours on the road to my new home for two to three months. My father in-law volunteered to transport me to Woburn Massachusetts to the Rehabilitation center to be retrained for regular life skills. We arrived at two thirty and were greeted by the staff at the entrance. We met with the team that were going to help me back to "normal." The new normal.

Checking in getting settle to my new home, away from home. My roommate a young kid full of piss and vinegar. A 2,000lb bail of paper fell on him and left him paralyzed from the waist down. Jeanne put my clothes away and it was time for them to leave, with a four-hour drive back. As I watched them leave, the thoughts of why me? Why not someone in jail or some drug addict who's a loser. I could see Jeanne crying and her father trying to comfort her. I was pushed back to my room to hang out with my roommate. My first night sucked! I couldn't sleep, God sends angels, and this angel was in the form of a nurse. She had married a quadriplegic. We had a long conversation that lifted me out of my silo despair. There would be many angels on this journey.

Monday morning "rise and shine", physical therapy started this is a different kind of boot camp. I was going to show them, but to my surprise I wasn't as strong as I thought. One pound on the pulleys was much harder than I expected. I have no balance, I can't move my arms up and down, my hands are useless, they don't work. This isn't just a challenge this feels impossible. The schedule is laid out five a.m. "bullet time", time for suppositories up the butt and take a dump. Every day give it a break, I know I'm full of shit but we negotiated every other day. What the hell, I want to do this myself, they look at me like this guy is going to be a challenge. I think he just doesn't get it. Another win the occupational therapist found my suppository holder that I could use myself. Small win but it keeps me working at it. Another Angel.

Showering was a different story, I liked it when the nurse would help, the first two showers were great, but they won this time. You can do showers yourself. Breakfast push your way down the hall to the elevator line up at the long table, like going to a wedding reception. These beautiful candy strippers would take our order and bring us our food. Another challenge holding a knife, fork, and spoon. Occupational Therapy to the rescue, "how about a fork holder." Nope, so for two hours we worked at trying different holders. Wedging the lightest fork between my fingers that would work and still does.

Now, on to catheterizing myself, this was tough. I did not want a piss bag hanging on the side of my leg smelling like fermented wine. It took a hand splint and a pair of clamps to shove the catheter up my penis. Yeah it worked, they took a video to show other people how to do this. Now my penis made the big screen.

More and more angels came into my life. In between all this "fun" I would make trips around to other rooms to help put a smile on others faces or go back to my room and pick on my roommate. This was called free time till lunch then followed physical therapy. Work the pulleys, balancing on a mattress, push-ups, rolling from side to side, working on how to dress, and putting on socks. All stuff that we take for granted. This was important stuff, so I could be as independent as possible. I didn't want my wife to have to do all this stuff. She had enough to do, working, managing the house and the kids. After therapy there was a group meeting to talk about our day. The rest of the day was free style I worked really hard on the weights and after some time I worked up to 25 pounds on the pulleys. Occasionally I would need to be pushed back to my room by my trainer.

Time to cook, Chef Roberge. Not quite start with eggs, two eggs on the counter and crack them into the pan/ Wedge the egg between my fingers drop into the pan splashing everywhere and the other eggs falling on the floor. Executive decision how about boiled eggs, not quite, getting the water into the pan and then the stove and later grabbing the hot pan. This created a real mess. Toast worked. Frozen food worked.

Always some trick with my buddies. Dropping food between our legs so the Candy Stripper Ladies could rescue it and clean the mess we made... It didn't take long for them to figure out that trick. Good while it lasted.

Jeanne would visit and notice my progress, things were going well. I still had to use a push chair until the insurance and fundraisers bought me a power chair. Field trips to the grocery store to shop with my buddy Ralph we had a great time. We had $40 apiece and we bought more junk food than household goods.

Now I've been in rehab for two months and I can feed myself, dress myself, catheterize myself, the team decided it was time to plan a trip home, to see what modifications I will need at home. Home for a weekend excitement and apprehension all at the same time. My father in-law picked me up to transfer me to my bed and my halo shifted and the front pins went into my skull. The halo was over my eyes, so I had trouble seeing. I felt like Robocop. This was not quite the weekend I had hoped for.

When I got back to the Rehab Center, they called the doctor to reposition the halo, so I could see. I wasn't exactly cooperative and kept pushing him away because I knew there was going to be some pain. I ended up in Boston and they put a new halo on my head. Two weeks later they decided the halo could come off. My buddy Scott picked me up at the Woburn Rehab Center and took me to Hanover to see the doctor and remove the halo. When the doctor took the halo off, my head fell to the side and Scott grabbed my head and the doctor put on a collar to support my head until my neck muscles could get stronger. That was a great moment. I went home for the weekend with no bars hanging in my face it was awesome. I could have hugs without bars in my face. My kids were so excited giving me their first real hug and kisses without the bars. My buddy Scott (another angel in my life) picked me up Sunday and I smiled all the way back to the Woburn Rehab Center. It was a great weekend.

Another trip by the Woburn team to see what changes needed to be made, they believe I am ready to go home. The changes seemed substantial, enlarge the bathroom, widen the doors, and change the toilet and a bigger shower. The ride back to Woburn seemed long and saying good bye to the kids and Jeanne became harder and harder. Would this merry go round ever cease? I just wanted to stay home. Another delay now we had to get more money for the changes. The support my buddies Scott and Bob provided was awesome, they wanted to take me out to eat. We decided to go to a fancy place. I had to go to the bathroom, but I needed some help with the process, so Scott and Bob are in the stall helping me catherize. A person came in and sees Scott holding my thing while Bob was shoving the catheter in. Poor man turned and ran out the door. Boy did we laugh. It was a great meal and a great time.

At long last it was my final week. One night everyone was bored so I decided to take all the friends I made that were patients there and go down to the fun room. We were having a great time until the nurse set the alarm off because she couldn't find us. We all hid in the corner and shut the lights off. She heard us laughing and came in screaming at us and sent us back to our rooms. It was clear I needed out, the nurse was still yapping and said when I found out who did this is in trouble. I told her it was me so stick that in your report. The best part of this was despite all I had experienced I was still myself at the core.

Two weeks left and I'm going home. All the work at the house needed to be completed before I could leave. I felt like I was in prison. I wanted to go home, I missed my wife, kids, brothers, and parents. Finally, the work was done at home. Scott had Friday off and gave me a ride home. When we pulled in at home everyone was there to greet me. I felt so good inside to see everybody, and to be home with my family.

Chapter 4

DETERMINATION, PERSEVERANCE AND ATTITUDE

NOW BECAME A new test. Being home was good, but it was tough on Jeanne, the kids adjusted as kids do but Jeanne took some time. She knew the road was going to be bumpy not smooth. She was patient and would listen to me talk about what I wanted to do. Big ideas about hunting, fishing, doing things with the kids. She would support me with my ideas even if she knew that it was going to be a process.

My BIG IDEAS were put on hold, when I realized I wasn't strong enough to do a lot of activities like before. My brother and friends (more angels) helped getting my toys ready to adapt for my disability. I started therapy at the hospital to build up my muscles working on pulleys three days a week. I joined the Special Olympics. I was involved with shot put, bench press, and power wheelchair racing. We had the game at University of New Hampshire. My buddy Chris came with me for that weekend. My first competition was weight lifting. We arrived at the weight room and waiting for my first lift. We had three. My first lift was 190 pounds. My competitor was big and looked mean he lifted 195 pounds and puts his fist in my face and says, "You're going down!" I was nervous, now it's my turn I have them put 210 pounds and made it no problem. The other Olympian tells them to put 215 pounds and he doesn't make it. My final lift I had them put 220 pounds to lift. I pushed up hard was almost there and I could feel my arms getting weaker, but then I thought of the other guy beating me. Boom, I made it and I screamed yeah baby. It was his turn and he had them put 222 pounds and failed. After his lift he was walking right at me and I'm getting nervous thinking he was going to hit me. He grabbed my hand and shook my hand and said "see you next year." So, working three days at a local weight lifting club and workouts at the hospital paid off. Sometimes I wanted to skip therapy and weight lifting club, but I'm glad I stuck with it.

The wheelchair race was fun. We would line up on the running track and the lanes. The lines at the end measured 25 yards and that was the finish line. Again, best out of three races. I lined up with three other racers, the gun goes off I pop the huge wheelie on two wheels and fly down the lane and land the win. When I popped the wheelie on the start, the man who fired the show thought I was flipping my chair over. He ran to save me and fell and sprained his wrist and had to be brought to the medical tent. So the next two races I was told to keep the wheels on the ground. I won the next two races and took GOLD. One event left, the shot put. I took Bronze, I didn't stand a change this guy in a wheelchair, had hulk Hogan arms and threw that 8-pound ball 25 feet farther than me. He kicked everybody's butt in that event. I went home with two gold medals and one bronze.

On the way home we took two Olympians with

us for the ride home. One of them was telling me that the kids at school tease them all the time and that's not fair. I told them to stand up for yourself and tell them what you think. Several weeks later at a Berlin meet he approached me with a big smile to say he stood up to the kids. I felt good inside and smiled the rest of the day.

During hospital visits the doors were manual and I had a hard time opening them. This was all before American Disability Act (ADA) regulations. I had a meeting with the Administrator and mailed out one thousand envelopes asking for donations to install electric door openers. Within three weeks we had enough money to put electric door openers at each entrance.

During therapy one day a rep from the brace Company offered me an opportunity to walk with their braces. After weeks of fitting for bracers it was time to try them out! I was a little dizzy at first standing straight up, but I felt really tall even if it took three people to get me strapped in and standing in the balance bars. It was hard, but I did it. I looked like a robot with cables hanging everywhere. My shoes were a size 15, I had to swing my hips to get the cables to pick up my leg to move forward. I would walk 6 feet and be so exhausted from the walk I walked two more times, but I didn't like it. Jeanne and I and the therapist decided to return the bracers. I sold my shoes to a basketball player.

Chapter 5

Keep on Keeping On – The Challenges The Rewards

Building my strength so I could hold my shotgun, drive a vehicle, and make it easier getting around in my push chair. My driving control was in and it was time for Norm to DRIVE. The instructor who lives at Crotchet Mountain Rehab Center 50 miles from my home. My buddy Dennis and his girlfriend drove me to his place. He installed my driving device at his home and I drove away happy. I had the biggest smile all the way home. I felt that I had gotten part of my independence back. I wanted to drive all the way home, but I was getting tired, so Dennis drove the rest of the way. Thank you, Vocational Rehab, for working hard with me to see what my capabilities were. There was a lot of testing, and after it was all done, they said I would be a good office worker. I laughed at the results. Being paralyzed is not a picnic, you want to do everything yourself, but you can't.

Now, that I had the ability to drive, I was able to pick my daughter up after school, run errands for Jeanne it was great.

Next challenge I had to find a way to shoot a shotgun. Once again Dennis to the rescue. He had a hand the size of Andre the Giant. He helped me with fitting the shotgun to my needs. Dennis lived next door so every day he would visit me and beat me at every video game we played. The days I would beat him he would trip me out of my chair and leave to go home to have lunch. He would say, be in your chair when I get back, so I can beat you again. And that he most of the time did.

Getting back to hunting was a challenge. We needed a way to help pull the trigger. First, we tried a loop of string sewed into a mitten. That didn't work. Then we welded a metal one-inch screw to the trigger. That worked. I joined a skeet shooting club to practice shooting. I was averaging 15 to 22 skeets a meet. My brothers Leo and Don were so excited for me. They were still not adjusted to seeing me in a chair. I could see it in their eyes, there was a beginning possibility of Duck hunting.

Next phase we had to build a Blind. How are we going to get me out to the bog to hunt? The blind had to be big enough for me and Dennis to hunt from. It took several days to build it was awesome. The Blind is in the backyard ready to go. Now, for the field trip to the bog. Where to put the Blind? My buddies decided to carry me out to the spot where I wanted to hunt. It wasn't bad getting me to the spot. But getting the Blind out there was crazy. They had me placed on a pile of brush while they carried the Blind to the spot. When they put the Blind down somehow the pile of brush shifted, and I rolled down into the swap. They left me there until the blind was stable. The way back was muddy, and they dropped me four times in the mud. Boy did we all laugh. The final technique was gripping me by my arms and dragging me out of the swamp like a dead deer. When we got back into the truck, we had mud everywhere and we laughed even more. Back to the drawing board for a better way to get out there and back. As we were leaving for the day a big flock of black ducks landed right in front of my Blind. This was very exciting. They decided to buy an old wheelchair and modify it with two six-foot steel pipes and carry me like an Egyptian Pharos. It wasn't pretty, but it worked.

Opening day of duck hunting was a success. I shot two blacks, one male woody, and two teal. What a great day. At the close of duck season, I tallied 34 ducks and two Canadian geese. I was happy.

Hunting season was over my buddies stopped by to see if I want to go for a ride up Cates hill to look for deer. Because the season was over it was illegal to spot a deer using a spotlight. We loaded up in my four-wheel drive Jeep Wagoneer and headed up Cates Hill to spot deer. As we drove by the Sugar House we ran out of gas. The guys were going to leave me in the vehicle while they went and got gas. Norm you stay in the vehicle while we get gas. I said no fucking way I'm staying here alone. No way! They took out my push chair and I got in and started back toward home. Two make it faster one of them stood on my anti tip bars on the back and the other sat on my lap. We were rolling down the hill at a good speed, snow on the road, we flew by the cemetery and now the front wheels are shaking. We came to Bryant corner and the chair tipped over and all three of us lying in the middle of the road covered with snow laughing.

Winter is the worst, as snow falls and cold weather sets in, I'm home bored and it's too cold to go out. We tried going to the Movie Theater and the Movie Theater was cold. Two days later two o'clock in the morning I'm sick my stomach and leg is swelled up like a watermelon. My brothers Leo and Don carry me out of my house on my mattress and into the van. Sicker than a dog off to the hospital. Thank God for my brothers.

Chapter 6

ADA –
Ahead of the Time

THE AMERICANS WITH Disabilities Act (ADA) prohibits discrimination against people with disabilities in several areas including employment, transportation, public accommodations, communications and access to state and local government programs and services. As it relates to employment, Title I of the ADA protects the rights of both employees and job seekers.

As you can see above the ADA was not limited to employment discrimination it also addressed and raised multiple questions as to why public funds were being invested in services that did not extend to people with disabilities, there is a strong similarity between the ADA of 1990 and the Civil Rights Movement of 1960's. It is interesting to note that once the question is raised the solutions while not simple seem so obvious. Questions very similar to the questions asked during the development of the original Civil Rights Act of 1866 which was the first federal law to define citizenship and affirm that all citizens are equally protected by the law. In this earliest movement the thrust was to offer protection to slaves freed in the aftermath of the Civil War. The purpose of the Civil Rights Act of 1964, one hundred years later, was to end segregation in public places and ban employment discrimination on the basis of race, color religion, sex or national origin. This was considered one of the crowning legislative achievements of the civil rights movement.

The ADA not dissimilar from the Civil Rights Act expanded the rights of individuals with disabilities in all areas of public life including jobs, schools, transportation and all public and private places that are open to the general public. The purpose and intent of the law is to make sure that people with disabilities have the same rights and opportunities as everyone else. The ADA is divided into five titles (or sections) that relate to different areas of public life. Title I Employment, Title II Public Services, Title III Public Accommodations, Title IV Telecommunications, Title V Miscellaneous Provisions. As with many broad sweeping legislative changes 28 years later we are still trying to test the intent and practical application. This has not been a simple journey.

Norm was born in 1957 and his injury occurred when he was twenty four years old nine year prior to the ADA. It is important to note that his achievements were herculean based on the traditional expectations of that era. He was a pioneer role model for the coming years and breaking into new ground rules as the ADA began to embrace the needs of individuals that experienced life changing challenges. He faced his challenges head on and was frequently challenged by laws and implementation that did not yet exist. His spirit and determination for normalization in a world that barely accepted his condition as normal. Perhaps although not official, individuals that experienced spinal cord injuries were active in expansion and development of the independent living movement of the 50' and 60's. The history of the independent living movement stems from the fundamental principle that people with disabilities are entitled to the same civil rights, options and control over choices in their own lives as people without disabilities.

The history of the independent living movement and its driving philosophy also have much in common with other political and social movements that flourished in the late 1960's and early 1970's. It is easy to state that society and social stigmatism existed in full bloom during this period of time and struggled to advance beyond common stereotypes. This combined with the de-institutionalization movement was and continues to be an effort to move people, primarily those with developmental disabilities out of institutions. Here in New Hampshire we saw the process of deinstitutionalization front and center with the closing of the state school in Laconia. Barely, prepared socially or practically, individuals were released to a society ill prepared. Did this actually create further struggles within the culture of 'what is normal'? The self-declared independent movement of young, primarily male, individuals who may have been 'normal' days prior were quick to define their needs for self-serving exclusive rights and not part of other social efforts of human rights for all. SCI's (spinal cord injured), rapidly promoted their needs being seen as the select few. Although recognizably being saved from catastrophic injury to become incarcerated in Nursing Homes designed for the old and feeble. Medical science frequently had advanced beyond traditional expectations of saving lives, only to create a more than dismal outcome. It is also fair to say legislative and politically society had advanced to a new platform of need and recognition.

As Norm and others in similar situations, continued to struggle for inclusion, social awareness was also reluctantly recognizing these efforts. It is fair to say that without the strong mindedness of individuals with spinal cord injury these changes may have been significantly delayed. The continued efforts for re-education and employment were struggles felt by many. Traveling through Norm's journey of perseverance to test these new opportunities, many of which were not prepared for the challenges in education, employment and transportation. Our heritage as a free society for equal rights is commendable and shines brightly in this brief but moving story of determination and resolve.

Attitude, attitude, attitude is the enlightened commodity of our heritage as a country, gradually winding its way through the struggle and recognition of meeting the needs of all.

This was not a linear movement, at least five parallel and transformative social movements influenced and energized the disability rights and independent living movement during the second half of the 20th century. A further journey into the heroic efforts may pose the question as to why Norm would subject himself to so many challenging situations. The reality is that it is frequently the young male that adventures into life with an indomitable desire to test or experience life to its fullest. Occasionally, the resulting challenges may be more threatening. In Norm's situations these new challenges did not deter him from experiencing life to its fullest.

Chapter 7

Technology to the Rescue

It's December and cold. My day is brightened with the knowledge that my power wheelchair will be delivered. My palms were raw from pushing my manual wheelchair around. The weather did not cooperate, and the delivery was postponed to Thursday. The delivery process and adjustments and instructions took two or more hours. I just wanted to cruise around the house and yell FREEDOM AT LAST!

I needed more room to move around so I took the chair outside there was a dusting of snow. A few spins around on the walkway, and right into a snow bank. It took the whole family to pull me out. Jeanne restricted me from snow excursions.

The wheelchair company wanted their money. My brother Leo and Don got together with the Milan boys and put on a demolition derby and the proceeds went to pay for my chair. It was awesome and everyone had a great time. Thanks guys.

It takes a village and Vocational Rehab in Berlin were outstanding when it came to assisting with all the adaptions for my disability. The bathroom needed a lot of work, and friend would come up to the house after a hard day at work and put me in the tub three times a week. Vocational Rehab helped with a new bathroom with a wheelchair shower and a bigger bathroom. I think Gary was as happy as I was. It felt good to take a shower by myself. Transportation was a problem. My jeep Cherokee had no room for my power wheelchair. Now what was I going to do. I notified my counselor from V.R. to see if they could help get me a van with a lift and driving device. After several meetings with Jean, I was approved to get a custom modified van. Yahoo! Things were falling into place. Each time things got better it would take pressure off Jeanne. Thank god she loves me. It took two months to get the van ready for me. Another BIG DAY. The van is parked in the driveway ready for Norm to drive. I took the family to the Dairy Bar for an ice cream. The simplest of things, like getting in and out of the van without any help.

Spring is here, and Jess is riding her bike and Nathan is riding his bike, neighborhood kids are all around. We had great neighbors.

Once a week I would take the kids to Gorham. They had BMX racing in Gorham it was awesome. Jessica was winning races, Nathan was winning races in the big wheel class. The boys on the hill were kicking ass at the BMX racing in their age class it was so exciting my brothers and I decided to build a BMX track at Jericho Park. By the end of the summer Jericho Park had a BMX track for the kids in Berlin. We finished with 15 riders but the following year we had 35 riders registered for that first race. We traveled the New England bike association circuit for two years and decided to stop doing it due to insurance prices for the track. We were hoping the Recreational Department would take it over, but that did not happen. That's Berlin. Well, it's the end of September and that meant duck hunting is coming.

Chapter 8

ANOTHER CHANGE IMPROVEMENTS FOR HUNTING AND OTHER CHALLENGES

AFTER GETTING SICK two years in a row I decided to buy some land on Route 16 about a quarter mile from my blind. So, the rest of the summer we built a 24 foot by 24 foot hunting camp. It was awesome, we had heat, shower, electric, water, cooking stove, fridge, and a king size mattress. October 3rd was two weeks away and I was ready I wanted to go to camp earlier than everyone else. I went up three days before everyone to settle in before they got there. It's October

2nd and the crew all check in. We decided to go to our blinds to sit and see what the night flight would be. We had ducks landing everywhere it was super. I couldn't wait to get back to camp and hear what the other guys saw. Everyone had a story of ducks flying everywhere. After a big meal for supper it was time to go to bed, so we can be fresh and alert to shoot some ducks in the morning.

The prior year I had called the recreation department to see if there was something I could do for the winter. They needed a 3rd and 4th grade basketball coach. Not knowing anything about basketball I took the challenge and became the Marston Magicians coach. My first practice I had an assistant who was a pastor. It was tough not swearing in front of him when the kids messed up. One time I said God damn and he was on the side of me giving me that look. I responded with Gods building a damn. He laughed.

Coaching that year was a great experience. I learned that kids accepted my disability better than grownups. By the end of the basketball season I understood the game. The accessibility and parking was awful at the recreational department. One time I was late to the game because someone who wasn't disabled parked in the handicap parking spot. Right before the game I went out to the center of the court and read the plate number and asked the person to stand and when he did, I asked him if he was with someone disabled. He replied no, and I said did you see the sign he said yes. Then I put my hands up and wheeled back. Accessibility was bad in the 80's. Shopping on Main Street sucked, restaurants were bad and no respect for the handicap signs. Coaching made the winter fly by. Winter is here again and I'm ready for another year of coaching basketball.

This year I had Nathan on the team and our next-door neighbor's son. We ended up winning the Berlin 3rd and 4th grade tournament. At the end of the season I was excited because I helped these little guys believe in themselves and take them to the top.

Spring was coming, and we were planning a fishing trip a place called Greeno Lake with Dennis and some other buddies. It was a big lodge and plenty of fish to catch. We fished after lunch and caught several brook trout and one 7lb Laker, not bad for the first day. We left early to fish and while we were trolling, by buddy hooked on to a monster, here I am sitting in the bow of the boat watching him reel in this fish. The fish is close to the boat and he's yelling "Get the net! Get the net!" he pauses and realizes that I was unable to get the net and help him. The fish jumps out of the water and snapped his line and the monster got away. I felt so bad, this guy was there for me any time I needed, and I let him down that day. I hated my disability for the rest of the day. I stayed in the camp and let them fish without me.

We packed up and left that night to go home. I decided to stop fishing after that trip. My buddies tried to get me to go again but it was a no.

School was out, and I was offered a job running outdoor camp at Jericho Lake for the summer, I took it for the challenge. The age of the kids ranged from 7 years old to 15 years old. The first week was crazy, everyone wanted to fish at the same time. After putting worms on their hooks and helping them cast. It was fun watching these kids do something they never did before. Not one kid wanted to take their fish home, they released everything they caught.

The kids swam a lot, we had a problem with blood suckers, and every kid at camp had a chance to pull off a blood sucker from their feet. The overnight was on a Thursday night. We told ghost stories, cooked marshmallows on a stick to make s'mores and watched movies. The kids loved it. It was tiring but worth it. I did this for five weeks it was fun and a learning experience working with younger children.

A team mate and i set up a schedule for the next year summer camps. And before the year was up we had 29 kids signed up for the next summer. Now I'm thinking they really enjoyed camp and my disability did not bother any of the kids. I was excited for next summer. The winter was tough, we had a lot of snow and cold weather. In the house every day without going out was depressing. I went out and played with the kids for fifteen minutes then I was freezing and had to go in. Sitting by the window watching Jeanne, Jess, and Nathan building a snow man in front of the house. It wasn't easy watching them, I wanted to be there with them. Life is starting to suck being in this chair dealing with the elements of Mother Nature. Spring was 1 month away.

The snow is gone the sun is out, and the grass is getting greener. The kids were in school, so I was alone and bored. I could hear music coming from a neighbor's house down the street from me. I look out the window to see who's there. I noticed activity down the street. They were talking in the driveway, so I decided to go visit them. I left my house in my electric chair wheeling down and I decided to release the clutches and freewheel to go faster with the chair. I was gaining speed and I couldn't push the clutches back in. Now I'm speeding down the middle of the road, shocked and heading for the rear end of a parked car. I couldn't scream for help, I'm fifteen feet away from smashing both legs and out of nowhere a neighbor grabbed the handles of my chair and stopped me from crashing into the rear end of the car. I was so thankful for him. He said I could see you coming but you weren't turning into the driveway and your eyes and mouth were wide open. I said he's in trouble and ran out there and caught you before hitting the car. I push in the clutches and wheeled over to the neighbor's house. Thankful once again for this unsolicited rescue. Sometime I do things before thinking of the consequences.

At last winter is over, the kids are out of school and off to Old Orchard Beach for the first week of summer.

This year good friends came camping with us, it was quite a week. The first day we decided to go to the beach, the whole family went out. We found a place that I could see them on the sand and I was on the sidewalk watching them. I tried to go on the beach, but the sand was so deep that it was impossible. It wasn't so bad, I had access to pizza, fried dough, and diet Pepsi in my cooler, and hot looking girls walked by. Its 2:30pm and its time to go back to the campground and swim in the pool till supper. After supper, time to have a campfire and cook s'mores, they were good. We are all sitting around the campfire and the garbage bag is moving. A cautious check and a yell "skunk! Get out of here before you get sprayed." I couldn't move because the chairs were in my way. So here comes that skunk right at me, he walks under my chair and stopped. I'm thinking please no leg spasms while he's under there. I could smell him bad. He stayed there for 5 minutes and eventually walked into the woods. That was the longest five minutes ever. No family support there. They were five campsites away laughing!

The next day we headed to fun town for the day. The kids were having a great time using the water slide, roller coaster, and playing games to win 50 cent prizes. It was hot, and the place is paved and that increases the heat. It was time for me to go back to the campground to cool off. Another fire at our place that night and a quick check of the garbage bag before starting the fire. The rest of the week was so hot, it was better for me to stay at the campsite while Jeanne and the kids were at the beach. We did the pier tour and it was crazy.

Everywhere we went the wheelchair was in the way or no access, sometimes I'd stay on the side walking dodging people as they walked by, while the family shopped in the store. At one of the stores near the bumper car's I asked the owner where the ramp was. He replied, go next door and shop he has a handicap ramp. I told him to stick it up his ass! Handicap, who gave us that name? I'm a handy man and I wear a cap? How about the sign, an outline of a person in a wheelchair? I don't need to be reminded that I'm in a wheelchair, give me a break. Back to the campground to relax because tomorrow we pack up and go home. That's the worst part when we get home Jeanne and I empty the camper, do the laundry and close it up till next trip. First week of Jcricho day camp next week.

Before my day camp started I went and bought a 17 foot bass tracker boat, so I could go bass fishing. The thing about this, I bought this without figuring out how I was going to get in the boat and use it. The first day with the boat I had figured a way to get in and out by myself, but someone had to drive my chair away from the boat. We used my boat that day to give rides to the kids on the lake, it was awesome.

Chapter 9

Day Camp

Here comes the recreation bus filled with kids aging from six years to 14 year of age. I have an office in the back of the outhouse where the backup water tank, holding one thousand gallons. The kids fished and swam the first day. We were busy with the amount of kids we had. Thursday was the overnight and I'm putting away the groceries we bought for the office. As I was putting away the hot dog buns, this loud bang on the side of me and water started shooting right at me. It felt like a fire hose. At one time I lost my breath due to the water pressure in my face, I'm screaming for help, but no one heard me. I was panicking of the fear of drowning; the water pressure was strong, and I could not move. I'm crying and drowning at the same time. Finally, a kid was coming over to get a fishing pole, he saw my struggling with the water. He went and got help to stop the water from spraying all over me. 10,000 gallons of rusty smelly water destroyed my electric chair. I had to be pulled out and carried to my van and my chair needed to dry. We dried the chair and turned it on and it worked. I went home and took a shower then went back to the park.

The maintenance crew was there fixing the problem. A pressure valve popped off. That valve would have killed me if that would have hit me in the head. I had trouble sleeping that night. I'm saying to myself "why me?" What did I do to deserve all this torture of mishaps? Well I laugh it off and had a great time with the kids the rest of the week. 4th week of camp my chair started giving me trouble, the kids and I were on a scavenger hunt and it started to rain. We started toward the hut and my chair died. We put the chair in neutral and the kids were pushing me every way but the right way, we were laughing so much. They were slipping and falling in the mud while pushing me to the hut. It was raining cats and dogs. We finally make it back to the hut and it stops raining. We sat in the hut laughing for ten minutes. The sun appeared, and the kids went swimming. We found a loose cable on my chair, plugged it in and it was ready to go. Then we packed them up and sent them home. On the way home, I was thinking the chair dies and the kids didn't hesitate to help me. All they wanted was to help.

Summer is over, and I were headed to Manchester to do some school shopping. I love shopping at the malls because every store is wheelchair accessible. Sometimes I get frustrated with the access up here, people have no idea how I feel. What I really hated was oh wait a minute I'll get help and lift you in the store. While they lift you, everyone is staring at you. One time I said to this lady, is there a bug on me, if there isn't stop staring. So, we shop until we had no more money and went home.

Chapter 10

OCTOBER HUNTING SEASON MY FAVORITE TIME OF YEAR

I PACK UP my clothing and hunting materials and off to the camp for two weeks. I was the first hunter at the camp, I was excited about duck hunting season, and we had all kinds of ducks swimming in front of the blind. The rest of the guys show up to hunt tomorrow. It was a crazy night and the morning came fast. We're in the blind and its dark and ducks are everywhere. The run rises and we open fire on the ducks in front of us. Cricket and I limited out in 25 minutes. We were back at camp by 8:00am we had breakfast took a nap and did a river run before lunch. A river run means taking a drive up Route 16 shooting at mergansers on the Androscoggin River. We shot ducks every day! I could have had more ducks, but I needed a dog. I had a record year, 42 ducks, 6 Canadian geese, two snow geese, and 22 mergansers. The best thing about this season is no mishaps yeah!

A big trip is planned for goose hunting in Maryland Kent County in January. My job was to map a route to Galena Maryland. We are using my van for the trip. After everything was in order to go. January was a week away and I was getting the he-be-jibe's. The guys were ready it's the night before and we decided to leave at midnight, it was snowing, and it was going to get worse, so we decided to go. i did all the driving 683 miles we stopped at a rest area on the way to take a quick nap. We drove on this bridge over the Delaware River it was so high from the ground, I was scared.

We arrived at the farm in the morning and gave us a key to a little farm house full of spiders. It was a shack in the middle of nowhere, surrounded by cornfields. We meet the guide and he tell u to meet him at the restaurant in town. I said is it hard to find, he replied "it's the only one in town." The population in the town is 245 people. That morning we meet the guide at the restaurant and we load up and off to the blind we go. Now I'm sitting in my chair in a plywood box with half a roof and a cricket sitting next to me in my blind. We could hear thousands of geese cackling getting ready to fly. I'm getting nervous they started to fly out of the water hole right over our heads my dream for a long time, I never thought I would get a chance to experience because I'm disabled. The guide says; ok take your safe off and get ready. Here comes over 100 birds but only shoot the birds at the end of the line. My buddies shot first, and I was so impressed with the birds falling from the sky from my buddies, I forgot to shoot. Here comes another group of birds and my cousin Rene and I were shooting at this group. Here they come I pick up my gun, put the sight about three feet in front of the first bird and fire the shot. The bird fold then I picked the one right behind. The one I killed and shot again and dropped that one and now there's one big goose at the tail end. We decided to go to Remington farm and shoot pheasants for the afternoon. A bead in front of that bird and fired and then dropped to the ground. The guide says; hey Rene good shooting, Rene replies that was Norm. I forgot to load my gun after the first shooting. He looks at me and says; damn boy, you can shoot! So, by noon time we had our limits 18 geese before noon. I felt so good that night everybody sharing their stories for the day. We went to bed early because tomorrow comes early.

We're back in boxes we were in yesterday and the sun was rising, and the birds were making that cackling noise and before you knew it, they were flying, and we were ready. Here comes a big group of bird's right at us. Lee says, "Ready now!" All four of us get up and shoot. Lee say's reload here comes some more, before he could say fire I started shooting and one of the birds dropped right in the blind. Boy did we laugh. It was ten o'clock and the birds stop flying so we were sitting in the blind half asleep and suddenly, boom and plywood from the roof everywhere. Cricket says, I was just checking to see if my safety was on. My ears were ringing after that for several minutes. We had him move to outside the blind the rest of the day.

We ended up with 16 Canadians that day, 2 shy of the limit back to the farm house for one more day of great goose hunter dream. This time we were hunting by the river which was cool, for me to get to the blind, for 200 years, I had to drive through 12 inches of water with my electric chair. It was windy and cold, and we are waiting for the geese to fly and all of a sudden fifty sixty ducks come flying in and Lee says go ahead shoot! All four of us start shooting for two minutes.

Straight and then it was nothing but screaming yeah baby did you see that! Between the dog and Lee, they recovered 35 birds. Boy! What a way to finish this trip, and its only 7:30am. By 9:30 we're ready to quit the birds weren't flying and we had a long drive home in the morning. Before I could say let's go a big flock of geese come landing in our decoys and we started shooting at them and six flew away out of twenty-two boy this trip is everything I thought it would be, but better. The trip home was fast and I had a freezer full of ducks, pheasants and geese. We book a trip next year and the year after that. My buddy Brian and I decide to go sea duck hunting on Delaware River, which was one hell of an experience itself. We met the guide at a marina that's not like a normal one. The boats were 10ft below the beam you walk to the ladder to get in. I had to get out of my chair and shimmy on my butt twelve feet out and then dropped onto my chair in the boat, a big oyster boat 50 feet long.

We get to the sport and the guide had 2 ropes 150ft long tied with 50 Clorox bottles space out on each. Brian and I shot our limit of sea ducks within 25 minutes, man was that great. When we arrived at the marina, they used a fork truck and some straps to get me out of the boat. Hunting to me isn't about killing, well the kill is a bonus, but it's about being outdoors. I can join in on conversations about dropping a goose or having thousands of birds fly over you, just being able to have an equal chance of hunting. Back at home I'm the guy who watches my friends sneak up to a flock of geese from the van because my disability holds me back from things normal hunters do. So, when I'm hunting in Maryland for geese, I'm not watching someone else shooting birds, it's me shooting birds, one of my last trips there, which was a great time I shot a buck with a 12 gauge at 100 years and it dropped right on the spot. My son Nathan was in a tree blind staring at flocks of geese flying over his head tree top high and two does walk right underneath him when he noticed they were a way away and he shot on of the two. Big brother Leo shot the other doe, Leo is a great shooter he seldom misses, and he is an awesome brother Don was too… All in the same day. Awesome getting an opportunity to share these special moments with my son and brother Leo that was our last trip to Maryland it was getting expensive the wife has had enough.

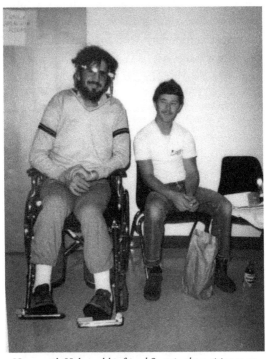

*Norm with Halo and his friend Scott in the waiting room.
This is the day the halo was taken off*

Norm shooting at some geese.

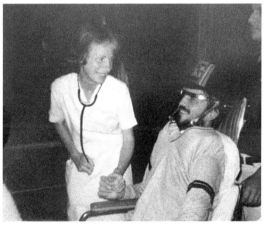

Nurse Betty as Norm is discharged saying goodbye and good luck

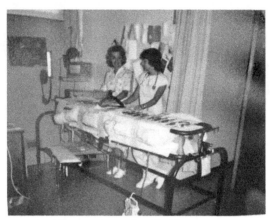

Nurses getting ready to flip Norm over – being flipped like a hot dog

Brother Leo, cousin, cricket, and others on Maryland hunting trip

Jeanne and family taking first vacation after the accident

Jeann and Norm at Special Olympics competition

*Jeanne and fried with Norm
at Special Olympics competition.*

Chapter 11

JASPER OF HILLSIDE NOT A SERVICE DOG BUT A HUNTING BUDDY

A NEW FAMILY member Jasper a golden retriever, 8 weeks old and cute! He had big paws with long fluffy legs. He would lay in between my chair legs and fall asleep. I would talk to him all day and him not saying a word in disagreement. I trained him to retrieve ducks he was a big golden 120 pounds, he was awesome if he could see or smell that duck it ended up on my lap. My friends would shoot a duck and Jasper would retrieve it and bring it to me. Ha! Ha! He was my best friend. Jeanne, Jessica, and Nathan loved him. He was a lot of extra work for Jeanne, but a great friend for our family.

Jasper was not like the Service Dogs of today. Once again some of the changes that have occurred developed well past the start of my injury. Service dogs today are custom-trained to assist people with physical disabilities affecting one or more limbs. They can enhance a person's independence by helping with tasks such as opening doors, turning light switches on/off or picking up objects. Service dogs are used to help people that have a variety of disabilities, and they frequently trained to assist when a crisis occurs.

Jasper was trained to assist me with hunting and was indeed a best friend. With training that is offered today he could have been a huge assist in many of the situations that I experienced throughout this journey to live my life to the fullest.

It is important to recognize and applaud the changes and progress that has been made socially. Acceptance and integration for individuals that have incurred physical, psychological, and a host of other disabilities. The contributions

Service Dogs have made for veterans, students and those with not visible disabilities has been huge.

Jasper indeed was a trail blazer along with me, helping and cheering me up on those long winter days.

Chapter 12

BEGINNING NEW CHALLENGES

COACHING SEASON WAS starting with 3rd and 4th graders. Nathan and the Marston magicians were going to have a great year. We were 9-2 going into the finals. I can remember Scott giving the referee the finger and the other coach breaking his pencil when Nathan scored. We caught this on video, it was funny. We ended up the champions that year. I would collect old trophies and fix them up. One for MVP, best defense, remembering to bring his sneakers, best team spirit, and showing up on time. We would have an assembly at Marston Elementary School and I would give a speech about the player and then I would call their name and have them come up and get their trophy. The whole school would cheer for that person. The kids loved it. I did this for two more years.

One day after basketball season Jeanne say's you should go back to college and get a degree in teaching. I laugh at that suggestion. Jeanne, was my support, advocate, and a great coach for me. I applied for a cleaning job at St Luke's Medical center where Jeanne works. They hired me to clean the lower floor 5 days a week I was excited I had a purpose.

I emptied all the garbage cans and wiped down all counter tops in every room. Do a toilet paper check along with tissues? Now it was time to vacuum that was a challenge between the power cord and the hose was a battle, but I managed. The first week was good. The second week went well everything was being cleaned but the vacuuming is still a battle between the hose tangling in my wheels or the hose hitting my control and sending me right into the chairs in the waiting room. One night the place was a mess. You could tell they were busy. My wife said they saw 24 patients that day.

It took me five hours to clean the place, an extra two hours. I locked the place up and pushed my way to the van. I brought down the ramp as I am heading for it I fell out onto the pavement. The wheelchair takes off. That night I had my push chair because my electric chair broke. I drag myself to the ramp and raised it up to the floor of the van. Now my chair is ten feet away and I have no clue what to do. I'm sitting on the edge of my ramp screaming for help, but no one is listening. I'm looking at my chair and thinking about my friend Dennis who died of cancer. I'm saying come on buddy help me out I know you're there! I'm looking at my chair and its moving my away and it stops close enough for me to reach it and get back in the van and go home.

When I got home and told the story to Jeanne, she looked at me like I was crazy. My electric chair was repaired and off to work I go. I have everything cleaned except vacuuming the floors. I started at one end of the building vacuuming the floor and suddenly, my chair takes off and smashes right into the wall my foot rest right through the wall and my tires are still spinning pushing my legs further in the wall. That's when

I noticed the hose was stuck on my control making it go forward. I pull it off and back my chair out of the wall. I tried to cover it with a chair but that didn't work, I left a note for the maintenance guy to repair it. After that incident, I made sure I was careful using that machine.

Winter settling in and its cold out and I must go to work, but because it's Friday I can go Saturday morning instead. The roads are clear and off I go. I finished working around 11:30 lock up the building and get in the van and started to drive around the building and I started to spin so I had to back up to get a head start, so while I was backing up, I hit the dumpster. I said no problem maybe a little dent, so I put it in drive and give it gas and the dumpster is moving with the van. I get out and here's a 3-inch shaft stuck in the back door of the van. The only way that it was coming out was to go forward until it works its way out. I'm back in the van ready to give it a try. I put it in low 2 and push the gas pedal to the metal and off I go. I'm looking in the mirror and the dumpster is still connected to the van. I stop and go again and the whole door pulls off and stays on the dumpster. I was so pissed off. By the time we were finished with this mess it was 3:30 I was upset. This is going to be expensive and a hassle with insurance. They paid it off and I moved on. This kind of work isn't working out, I smashed the wall again and they weren't happy with me. It was time to realize cleaning is not for me.

Now I'm thinking of all the programs I was running for the recreation department, it was awesome. I like working with kids. Jeanne and the kids were bugging me to go back to school and be a teacher. I kept thinking no way, I'm not smart enough for college. I went to vocational rehab and asked for some help applying for college. My counselor was awesome, she helped me with everything and was supportive of the idea. Vocational Rehab was there for me once again.

For me to get accepted to Plymouth state College, I had to meet with the Dean of the college next week on Tuesday 9:30am in his office. I had trouble sleeping all weekend thinking on what kind of questions he's going to ask me. Monday came, and I was trying to talk myself out of going tomorrow. It's Tuesday and I'm not driving to Plymouth thinking how nervous I am and I'm hoping I don't screw up this interview.

I'm sitting in his office waiting to meet the dean with Jeanne, he had degrees, awards, plaques having everywhere. He comes in introduces himself and sat down behind his big desk. He asked me to tell him who I was. What happened to me, and why I want to be a teacher?

After telling him who I was and how I ended up in this wheelchair and my goals. I also told him I wanted to get off Social Security. He looked right into my eyes and said welcome to Plymouth state college as a student. I had the biggest smile and thanked him, it was a quick ride home. Everybody was happy to hear the good news. Now I must get ready to move on campus. I'm glad I had a month to get ready. I moved into a family housing, but it wasn't accessible, the bathroom is small, and the kitchen is small. The maintenance came in and widen the door and added an access ramp to get in. When I'm leaving the building, I must drive down the driveway to get to the sidewalk, but I'll manage like always.

My final meeting with my vocational rehab counselor before going to school. She had everything organized, all the paper work was done and now all I needed to do was show up for the first day. I was so nervous about this. Two more days home and I'm off to school. Nathan was going to high school and Jess is going to a college in Vermont, and I'm going to Plymouth. This is going to be a crazy year.

Chapter 13

The Stretch

1ˢᵗ Day of School

8:30 and I'm off to get my schedule for the semester. There were students everywhere all my daughters' age. I get to the main building and there's a line all the way across the street. Not knowing anybody I was nervous and got at the end of the line. It was hot out and the line was moving slowly to the door of the building. I finally make it to the office and they are closed for lunch. I waited right there until lunch was over. The girl says your Special Ed you're in the wrong building. As I was leaving, I hear someone yell

Roberge over here, I look over and its Craig, I went to lunch with them. I felt a little better knowing some people. I found the sped office and a woman named Jeanne who was my counselor for school. We went over my schedule and she was there for me. I felt a lot better after meeting with her and what she could do for me.

That afternoon I went to see where all my classes were and settle in for the night. Tomorrow was orientation and I was so nervous. The next day was here and I'm off to something without my wife to help me. My first class was literature, the teacher gave his speech and started asking questions. He says what is literature? He picked me to answer the question. I replied to him and said, "That's when you buy a car and ask for the literature on it." The whole class began to laugh but the teacher replied saying "You're right, but that's not what I was looking for." He didn't ask me anymore questions that hour. I went to the rest of my classes for that day. The rest of the week I was busy getting books and finding the best ways to get to all my classes. Every class I went to the desk wasn't accessible I had to look over my notes one last time before class.

Its 8:30 in the morning and I have math at 9:00 I get to the class and the teacher says surprise math test, math was never my favorite subject. I took the test it took a little time, but I felt good about it. Science was next, I get there, and no one is there but a note left on the board that reads "take a packet on my desk and take it home, turn it in on Wednesday" I was excited! The take home test wasn't easy, it's Wednesday and it's time to go to math to see how I did on my math test, the teacher says five people passed and the rest of you will have to take it over. Twenty-two students in my class and only five passed no way I'm one of those five. He starts naming them off and the last one he names is me. I was shocked, and then the teacher says, you five students can leave now the rest of the class can take the test over. I left the class with a smile.

My next class is science again the teacher was absent, so we left our test on his desk and off to lunch. The next day I went to check my grades for science they were posted in the hallway of the class. My grade was 98, I was so happy. I was having a problem taking notes, so my advisor and I decided to try a tape recorder while the teacher talked. That didn't work so I needed to see the work to comprehend it. my advisor at school gave me a carbon copy paper and I would ask a girl if she could use the paper to take notes. It worked! I was excited to go home this weekend to brag about my grades. I hated to leave home on Sunday, I was feeling like I was leaving all our problems in Jeanne's hands, to take care of everything it's a lot of pressure on her thank God she was tough.

The weather is getting colder at college, the roads were freezing up, and the walkways were getting slippery. One morning I woke up and there was 5 inches of snow. I was leaving the building to go to my morning class, I had to drive down the driveway that had like a 50 degree slant down into the road and then had to go up the road to get to my class well as I started driving the electric chair down the driveway and the chair started to slide sideways and when it hit the bottom of the driveway, where the road connects the chair tipped and roles over, and I went flying out. The chair ended up on top of me, here I am laying on the side of the road people are driving by looking at me wondering what I was doing. Finally, a woman stops, she gets out of her vehicle she says "Mr. are you okay or are you doing exercise? I responded no lady my wheelchair rolled over on me could you please call 911. The ambulance pulled into the driveway and took care of me put me in a stretcher and drove me to the hospital to check and see if I had broken bones. Everything was okay no broken bones, so Craig and Jib show up with my van and pushchair to get home. My electric chair was demolished from the accident, it was a new chair. I had to call REQ which is in Manchester about one hour from Plymouth. Jan and Scott Soderquist, I started dealing with Jan when they moved from their garage to a building next to a state prison. It was awesome, you had to wheel up this long ramp to this big door then down a long hallway to her office and work area. Now they're a big company with a lot of people working for them. I had my push chair until REQ delivered me a new electric chair. In the meantime, my buddies had to push me around campus. It was a Tuesday morning it was 830 in the morning and Craig and I were going to be late for class because Craig did not set up the alarm clock that night, so I jumped in my push chair and of course it was snowing out as we were heading to the class we hit a hole and I went flying out of my wheelchair landing in the snow and Craig falls on top of me and we just laid there and laughed for about five minutes. Five minutes and then a student came by and helped Craig pick me up and put me back in the chair, it was hilarious. By the time everything was done, we were 20 minutes late for class. We decided to go back to my apartment and leave a message saying, "sorry we can't make it to the class, I had a problem with my wheelchair." I get a message from REQ my electric chair will be delivered tomorrow morning. Yeah! My electric wheelchair is delivered to the school that morning. It was great to have my electric chair. Once again, I'm on my own and I'm getting to class on time. This semester is almost over. Nathan played basketball and baseball this year and I hurt on the inside I wasn't there for his great moments and to support him on his bad times. The same with Jessica I felt I wasn't supportive enough with her also in her cheering and tennis playing. Jeanne had the biggest job of all, she was the dad and mom her responsibilities of taking care of the house, kids, to school, and to work 40 hours a week. I cried many nights thinking of what I left on Jeanne's shoulders at home while I was here trying to change my career. There were times when I stayed up late trying to understand what I read. I would study my notes for a test and go to bed confused. One time I thought about quitting but in the back of my head there was Jeanne, Jessica, Nathan saying dad don't worry you can do this.

I thought my grade point average would be bad, but I received a 3.1 out of a perfect 4.0. I was happy with that overall GPA for my first year of school is pretty good. I had to call Jeanne to tell her my grades. Going back home after my first semester was great but living on my own for 6 months, I had to adjust to the way of home life for the summers. It's the second week of august and were getting ready for school shopping, off to the malls we go. We spent a lot of money preparing the kids and I for school. My second-year is about to start and I'm excited, last year I was nervous and I'm excited, can't wait to meet all my new friends from last semester.

The first day of school is when you get to meet all your friends and you get your classes because being a second-year college student you didn't really go through what you had to go through the first year. Getting my schedule was pretty fast knowing and my finding my classes was easy. Heck this is like being in my backyard. I had a science class which was just awesome his name is Mr. O he was my age, so I felt like I had something over the younger kids in my class. We did a lot of hands-on and he always adapted his lesson to my disability. I enjoyed his class.

The month of September was great, my classes were going well, homework was easy, so I made plans with my son and nephew Keith, to take a ride up Androscoggin River and maybe shoot a couple of ducks on the way. Duck season had opened, and I didn't go last year and I had a long weekend coming, so we decided to go. From Milan to Errol we didn't see any ducks along the river. We decided in Errol to take a ride up to the border of New Hampshire and Maine, there are several good potholes on the way. As we were approaching the border there was one water hole left. Sure, enough we get around the corner of the horseshoe there they were. Canadian geese we were pumped! Keith and Nathan got out of the van and snuck down around the corner and down to embankment. I pulled up right on the side of camp and positioned myself to shoot from the van. I loaded up and had the gun pointed outside the window I took the safe off and the end of the barrel was resting on my elbow, than I noticed a Canadian goose was flying right at me, now my chance I reach down to grab the gun not realizing that the gun had flipped upside down so I pushed down right on the trigger of the shotgun and it fired and blew my left arm right out the window. Yeah! It was hell after that, my left arm was hanging out, blood squirting out, nerves and skin all over the windshield. I said to myself this is it, I'm going to bleed to death, I picked up my left arm and my forearm was hanging down and seeing it and not being able to move my hand and the bone hanging out of the top of the arm. After seeing that I was saying I'm going to die in front of my son and nephew. I started yelling for Nathan and Keith for help. Finally, my nephew and son heard me it took them several minutes to get there, they were out of breath from running out of the swamp.

Keith grabbed my forearm and put it on my belly. Nathan trying to maneuver me over from the driver's seat to the passenger seat. One of them is holding one part of my arm the other over my body with the stub of my arm and they're dragging me over to the passenger seat. I was in shock! I really couldn't feel any pain in my arm, it was just like a horror show. Blood all over the windshield, skin, fat on the mirror. Finally they get me to the passenger seat and drove to a store which was right around the corner not even 100 yards. They ran in the store and called 911, grabbed a bunch of bandages and a applied a tourniquet to keep me alive. It didn't take very long for the ambulance to get there they put me in the ambulance and off to Berlin I go forty miles away. The driver told me not to worry buddy we're going to get you there as fast as I can drive this rig. Before I knew it, I was in the hospital. It felt like it only took 20 minutes and we were a good hour away. Now, I'm brought into the emergency room and of course some of the doctors we knew. Here's half of my arm laying on the tray and the other half with bones hanging out, it was bad. My brother Leo comes in and looks at my arm and leaves the room, he went through hell when he was in Vietnam, so he started getting flashbacks.

The strongest one in my family there is my wife Jeanne she wasn't crying I can see her thinking and looking at me with her big black eyes. I could feel it inside her saying your hunting is over. So, the Dr. arrived and looks at my arm and says; we're going to cut the rest of your arm off, I looked up at him and said; no fucking way! I can't walk and can barely use my arm as it is. I want a second opinion, they decided to ship me to Hanover, so here we go again of 4 ½ drive in the ambulance.

We arrive at the emergency room and their ready for me. They brought me to my room and waited for the doctor to arrive. The Dr. comes in she looks at my elbow, then grabs my forearm and move it around dangling by my skin and I can feel her doing this, I was flipping with pain. She was like 6 feet tall, long jet black with the grey streaks in it and she had a big nose, she looked like the wicked witch of the north in the Wizard of Oz. She picks up my arm and says, I served 2 terms in Vietnam, I think I can repair this for you, I have handled worse, and she put a smile on my face and everybody else that was there. My family was happy to hear that. Okay so for the next seven days was hell. I was in the operating groom every day being worked on because it couldn't be done in one day. I was so doped up I didn't know who was coming or going.

Surgery 6 to 7 hours every day for a full week. Recovery was real tough to take I was worried about school, my family. I'm always putting my family through so many accidents. How much more can I and they take? I'm always in good spirits I'm always trying to smile but sometimes it sure is hard if you don't smile. Nobody else will. And in today's world everybody wants to be happy. We just need to be happy.

It was time to go home and heal so I could go back to school, the doctor advised me not to go back to school for the rest of the year. I didn't agree, I was in the middle of my third semester. My first idea was maybe I can talk to my professor to let me finish my classes at home. Two professors let me finish my class at home. Between the drugs and therapy my arm is getting better and better. I was determined to go back to school. The doctor said I really wasn't ready! I decided to go back for the spring semester after a big discussion with Jeanne.

Back to school without my pills, it was tough for two to three weeks having pain and nothing to take by my choice. Thank God for homework and studying for exams that made me forget about pain. Everything is going well with my classes than one night after class I hit a hole and ripped one of my front wheels right off the frame of my wheelchair. It took 2 hours to get back to my apartment after that I had to use my pushchair until it was fixed. Now I had to call for help to get to my classes for the rest of the week. Just when things are going well, I get kicked in the ass again. Why me? I ask myself, why me? A lot of areas aren't wheelchair accessible, but they think it is because there's a walkway? It's very embarrassing when you're sitting there with parts in your hand because the walkway had bricks missing. Most of the merchants aren't accessible in every town and cities in the state. If you want to feel the pain I do, take a chair in front of your favorite store and sit there while you watch your family shop in the store because it's not accessible. It happens to me a lot, people just don't understand.

3ʀᴅ Year at College with Jess, my Daughter.

Jessica decided to go to Plymouth state with me. She had her own place with friends she also played tennis for the college, I was proud. We had several classes together one of the classes was world history, I wanted to beat her so bad. My buddy Brian would travel from Alton Bay to visit me and help me with my studies. Sometimes I needed help so things would sink into in my brain. He would explain things better than my professors for me to get a better understanding. It was a great year my student teaching was in Belmont 4th grade, I had a great learning experience there, and the teachers were awesome. By having my daughter there was the best, being away for the family is tough but having her here with me was great! In our history class she and I ended up with a b+. The time flew by. Not that we hung out together but just having her there was comforting.

I had a great semester nothing broke and no accidents and good grades. Yeah!

4TH AND FINAL YEAR AT PSC

It was the end of August and it was time to pack up and head to school, my apartment at PSC was ready for me to move in. You get to see everyone from last semester. I had my classes set from the spring semester, so I was ready to do it, I had a full schedule and it was busy. The classes were busy but preparing for your student teaching for a whole semester was nerve wracking. My friend suggested an elementary school where she taught. I sent my paperwork at school requesting 4th or 5th grade, for my student teaching. Two weeks later I received a letter of acceptance to do my teaching in the 4th grade with a tough teacher, but a great one. I was happy. So, the rest of the year went by fast except at the end it was finals and the people living upstairs from me had a party at 2:00am. I called them and ask them to be quiet and they responded with "fuck you, you crippled bastard." I went home from that weekend to cool off from the week when I went back to campus someone had kicked in my window and trashed my room. I ended up traveling from home to Plymouth every day. There were two weeks of school left. I was upset about what happened at school and thought about getting my brothers to come down and kick their asses but decided not to. They weren't worth it. Graduation was exciting, thousands of people watching and waiting for their kid to go up and receive their Diploma. I was so nervous when they called my name and Jessica right after, everyone yelling as I rolled up to get my degree WOW! It felt good.

Chapter 14

BACK HOME – NOW WHAT?

THE SUMMER WAS hot, and I had an interview for a sub job at a school. There weren't too many openings for teachers that year and I wanted to work! I went for my interview and felt the other person who applied would get it being young it was a second-grade job. She got the job and I needed to move on, a few days after this was done, I get a phone call, it was the principal at the school, he wanted to know if I would take the second-grade job until the regular teacher comes back. Apparently, the person they hired got a permanent teaching job in the south.

I was excited to work. My first job was a challenge 2nd graders all subjects had to be taught. In science I decided to study the jobs of a paleontologist, I took a section of the classroom and turned it into dinosaur land. I had red paper over the lights reading books on paleontology and different dinosaurs. I incorporated spelling words, tracing dinosaurs on colored paper, and picking a dinosaur to write a short story about it. To top off this I buried plastic bones of the dinosaur in the sandbox and the students acted as paleontologist and had a great time! The teacher came back from maternity leave and I was done teaching. There was a teacher leaving soon but no one ask me to do it so my hope for that job was slim. So I decided to ask who was subbing for her when she leaves. She replied, "You are, I didn't get a chance to talk with you" So now I'm teaching 3rd graders for two months. I was excited to do this. Hopefully after this they might hire me full time if there an opening later on. It was great subbing for her, the kids were busy.

With everything going on at school they had a fifth-grade teacher who was on maternity leave after the holidays. I applied for it and by the time I was done subbing for the third-grade teacher, I was told by the principal I had the 5th grade position. Yeah!! Another teacher going out on maternity leave, three jobs in a row from maternity leave. But this third job opens a full-time job. 65 students in two classes was too much. The school board to break up the six graders into two classes' so when the teacher came back it was a surprise that the 6th graders were divided without her knowing anything. The principal didn't notify her at all. So, she thinks I had everything to do with it. She was mad at me for a while. I had a full-time job teaching geography and science, awesome I was pumped. Now I can get off Social Security and feel normal. We had three classes rotating every 85 minute period. My classroom was at the end of the building perfect I had access to the school yard for activities that go along with my lessons. I had a fish pond, lizards, frog races and fish. I had 5th and 6th grades. We had a staff meeting in the spare classroom after school so during the meeting I had to go to the bathroom there wasn't any accessible for wheelchair> I went to the next room to go pee. When I entered the bathroom the door behind me shut and there was no room to move. I was yelling for help back into the door hoping they would help me. 20 minutes go by and no one is wondering what that noise was or where is Norm? Finally, someone heard me yelling and she came into the room and realized I was stuck in the bathroom. So, we get back to the meeting and someone said where you been, I replied I was stuck in the room and they all laughed for 10 minutes. I was hurting inside that they laughed at me. Even the boss. I wanted to complain that there is no bathroom wheelchair accessible, but I did not because I was afraid to lose my job.

Four months left for the school year, and the summer off. I was ready to back to school at the end of July! The janitor's finish my room first so I could get an early start on fixing my room for the first day of school. It was awesome setting up my room for science and geography. I had my cousin come and draw dinosaurs and solar system on the chalkboard. He is the best when it comes to drawing. My first full year was tough, I had full classes, no time to go pee. Lunch was quick, and the bathroom was always busy. There was the student's bathroom also. The janitors made the stall door wider, so I could squeeze in with my electric chair and do a direct piss in the toilet. I would hear the funniest sayings from the kids taking a leak and them not realizing I'm in there. The bathroom for me was bad but I was afraid to lose my job that wasn't secured yet. I could not use the library because it was in the cellar with no access. I was okay with it the students would go down get what they need and do their research in the room with me.

Homework was a challenge for me, sixty-two students is a lot of papers to correct. I spent one hour a night correcting and recording it in a grade book. The spaces were so small it wasn't easy when you write big like me. There were several times a student would approach me and say Mr. R. you marked it right but it's wrong. I would reply because you were honest, I won't change the grade, but good job bud. So, I decided to take 10 minutes of class time and go over the homework with them that was easier for all of us. We had meetings every day in the morning and after school some of them useless. So, the rest of that year went by. Summer break was here, and I was getting ready for this fall.

I started to work on my classroom the first week of August setting up the desk was the easy party, but the bulletin boards were tough, thanks to my mother in-law for giving birth to Jeanne, she would turn my boring ideas to awesome poster boards. I also bought a fish pond instead of a fish tank for the classroom.

Finally, my room is ready, we start next week, and I was pumped! The first week was three days of useless meetings and two days of meeting my students and parents. Sisters and brothers of my students, it was crazy! I was teaching geography and science so I started with the five themes of geography and worked our way to states and capitals boy oh boy I ask the class, where is New Mexico located and the boss had his hand up so I picked him and responded with New Mexico is part of Mexico and before I could pull him to the side to correct him I had a student yell out "what's a matter, don't you know your states and capitals? New Mexico is in the United States, not in Mexico Mr. Principal!" The whole class broke out laughing at him when he left the room. It took 10 minutes to get them to focus back on states and capitals. I would pass out a study sheet on what capitals to prepare for a test. 15 states and capitals, 1 through 15 well the kids were studying them in the order of the list, so one week I decided to change the order of the words while giving them their test. I received several phone calls from parents saying it was wrong to change the order of the words. That was a crazy year. It was my first science fair with 52 kids. I had science boards and their projects everywhere in the gym. We packed the gym that night with parents, grandparents, aunts and uncles to see their kids' projects. The 5th and 8th graders were tired the next day. With the two classrooms so big I was glad to see April vacation around the corner. The rest of that year went fine.

That summer was hot, and I stayed at home to stay cool. August was here and time to set up the classroom. I bought a fish pond for the class it was 3ft wide and 5ft long and 2ft deep. Our first meeting of the year we took a break and soaked our feet in the pond. The third week started off with morning recess duty the exit to the playground is right next to my room so that makes it easier for me. I had mentioned to the janitor that the bottom of the ramp to exit had a three inch drop before hitting the pavement. Well the next morning I was bringing some first and second graders out to the playground as we were walking to the bottom of the ramp the little kids cut in front of me and the front tires twisted, and the chair tilted forward throwing me out of my chair tumbling down an embankment finally stopping.

I look up and the kids were staring at my legs because of the spasms I was having after the fall. I wasn't physically hurt but inside my mind that wouldn't have happened if someone had fixed it but there was always some excuse. I felt for the kids that were talking with me' they were crying thinking I was hurt bad' it sucked. I didn't want to complain about it I was afraid of losing my job. I was still using the boy's bathroom, it was really hard to go to the bathroom especially when two students come in talking about how much homework they have or a girl the boys like in their class. A father of the student I had in class one day mentioned Lego robotics competition he went to. He noticed the kids loved it. So I decided to get a few Lego kits and started several teams. These kids were working very hard on the mission, they didn't realize they were using math, science, geography, and good social skills to accomplish their mission. I incorporated it with the lessons I was doing in class. Some teachers didn't agree with the lessons I was doing in class. The teacher who taught across from my room was an awesome teacher the kids loved her and she gives love back. Sometimes we need to listen to the children and respond with a positive answer to show him or her you care. That was her approach to teaching.

Another teacher, would always yell at students for doing something dumb but if that kid needs help she was right there to help after yelling at him or her. She was also one of the best, she was tough on the outside but inside she was a buttercup.

It was October 16th heading to school it was raining heavy at the time. I'm approaching the ski jump and the van door opens and my lift drops while I'm doing 50 miles per hour. I pull over and the van door closes, but when I put it in drive it opens? So it was cold ride to school that morning.

Now I have to take a trip to Manchester to have them repair my van, $75,000 dollars and this is happening two months later, bullshit! The company came up to fix it because vocational rehabilitation told them they would hold back the last payment of the van. It's amazing how money talks. They came up on Friday. But Wednesday, Thursday, and Friday my wife had to help me in the morning. It bothered me inside that my wife had to help she's always helping me. I'm lucky to have a woman like Jeanne, I ruined certain parts of her life with mine, she doesn't show it but I can see the pain in her eyes.

We had a lot of snow that winter and spring was here and I love doing rockets with the student's, the lesson was on the three laws of motion. In the school yard with 30 rockets ready to blast the sky. I would invite the other classes to come and watch, and help with the countdown before each launch. The students should build their own rocket to launch. I would start to build mine and I would have a lot of trouble doing it, I would never ask for help, because I knew someone of my students were watching me and I wanted to show them I could do it. Well 5 minutes into it, a student came over and says, "I'll help you with your rocket and then you can help me finish mine. I gave in and we did them together. How thoughtful he was. Science fair is here again and I had a student whose little sister wanted to give me her presentation at seven years old. She had a board and an experiment to go with it. She was awesome. When she reached the 5th and 6th grade she was acing everything she did. Again the science fair packed the school gym it was nice to see everyone coming to see their child's work.

At the end of every year the school had a volunteer supper for science fair students. We have a new cafeteria next to the gym so the sixth graders set the tables and a table up front for rewards for helping. The kids put up a podium for the speaker but no microphone to speak. So my boss decides to hook up a microphone from the gym system. Everyone is sitting down and the teachers standing in the back. My boss head up to the podium and grabs the microphone and starts talking but his voice was coming from the gym. We laughed for ten minutes hard. We still laugh about it today. It's the end of school and that means field trip! Overnight at the AMC huts. These trips were awesome and yet frustrating. The awesome part that the kids get so much out of this trip. Educational and great social skills. On these trips you're not allowed to bring candy, but I would bring bags of candy and sneak in the kid's room when they were on a hike, and put candy in their bags. After supper I would tell the kids to stand in the hallway with their bags for a candy check. To see their face expression when they open their bags and find candy in it. Priceless.

The downside for me was that I had to stay at the base because my chair wasn't made for trails. I was okay with it, I'm there for the kids.

The new principal for the fall. I was excited about having a former teacher as the boss. She let me do a lot with the kids, like I was doing a unit on the rainforest. We decorated our hallways just like the rainforest it was awesome. I had doves in the classroom along with winter dragons and gecko lizard. We had a fire drill during this unit and the students had the lizards with them outside and one of them bit a student and would not let go. Eventually it let go. We all laughed about it after. I had two students that challenged me every day. Boy they were tough. I gave them challenges they would whip right through. These girls would help me prepare my materials for the next day, make my birthday cards for my wife and help me wrap my Christmas presents for my wife. These girls were best buddies until high school. She would have her mother drop her off at my school to hang out with me until her father would pick her up. She made a decision to go to a private school in the 10th grade.

I'm so proud of her being able to be away from her parents and maintain outstanding grades and making new friends and full scholarship for college. Great job girl! Her grandmother sometimes would sub for our nurse and she would walk in my room and I would say hi mom. After a while the kids were asking her if she was my mom. She retired from working in the emergency room at our local hospital. She knows me well from all my visits. Ha! Ha!

Our principal decided to go back to being a regular teacher the next year, so that meant a new boss. Which means everything going to change again. We were doing a unit on Egypt, and the kids dress up like the Egyptian and I have a diner like they did back then.

We had to make all food in class boy was it messy in my room. But I was watching the students, they were so involved in this project and working together. I had to help with the bread, I had two other students helping and I accidentally spilled some flour on the other students and they retaliated by throwing flour all over my head and the first thing you know the whole class is throwing flour on everybody, it was awesome we laugh. Over the years of teaching I've learned that students learn more from a hands on project with a little research on the web, than having them read from a textbook. According to the custodian, he would tell me all the time your room is the messiest of them all. Spring was here that meant science fair and spring vacation. This science fair was great, we had volcanoes, water cycle, and air measurements at different levels, dinosaurs, rockets, solar system, and many more. After spring vacation, it was time to meet the candidates for the principal job. The first guy I met was walking down the hallway like he had the job already, yeah! He was from Berlin, he had a few years as assistant principal at another school. The next candidate was out of state with no experience in being a principal of any school. He looked like Tom Brady, he seemed to be a nice guy. Well he got the job and everybody was happy.

September's here and school has started with the new principal. He's a hunter so that's pretty cool. I was working with the kindergarten teacher to combine the classes for our fish program. My fifth graders would educate the little guys on the life cycle of a salmon. We would get the eggs from a hatchery and have them in a special tank set up by the kids. It was cool, every day one little guy and one of the fifth graders would record the growth of the eggs in the tank. I also had a 50 gallon fish tank for goldfish, suckerfish, and silverback fish it was neat.

The last week of October my daughter called my wife crying she was trying to tell us she had breast cancer at level 3-4. My wife took a vacation flew down to help with everything while I stayed home because I could not get the time off and it was a long drive for me. I wanted to fly down but the airlines are horrible with wheelchair people. So the following year after she was cleared of cancer we drove down to Tampa for Christmas and surprised our grandchildren Emma and Luke.

We had this tank next to the window filled with fish and it was time to clean the inside glass, it was green. One of the students volunteered to clean it, great! He headed over to the sink and grabs a sponge to clean it. He did a great job! I'm in the middle of a lesson and the girls sitting next to the tank are screaming jumping out of their chairs. The fish were jumping out of the tank and dying on the floor. Within two minutes all the fish were wiggling to death on the floor. All the girls are upset, and the boys were laughing along with their teacher.

While this was happening my boss walks in to see what all the noise was. So the students decided to investigate this situation. Who the culprit was, without him knowing it. The janitor had used that sponge to clean our desk, and the same sponge was used to clean the fish tank. The tank was cleaned again and new fish were added.

Chapter 15

SADNESS WITH VERY FOND MEMORIES

THE NEXT WEEK was one of the worst ever. Sunday afternoon my brother Leo and Keith drive into my driveway to visit. I thought, oh good and wonder what they might be up to? I met them on my front lawn and they told me my brother Don had died in a motorcycle accident. I responded with okay where is he around the corner playing a joke on me? They weren't joking he had died. Don was a great brother, he would make everybody laugh. He was tough guy, I could tell you a lot of stories about him, and everybody knew Don! I'll share one story about Don.

We had to get some groceries for hunting camp. So we drove to Shaw's to get our supplies, we're getting out of the van and heading into the store and he stops to talk to a couple. While he was talking he jumps and lands right on top of my lap and tells them, we have to leave. We get around the corner and I push him off and said "what the hell is your problem"? He says, look down at your groin. I look down and my balls were hanging out. Don and I laughed all the way back to camp. A week later he sees the couple and the guy says; tell your brother he's got big balls. We laugh again. I miss him.

Needless but important to say, my brothers, my family, my neighbors and my community were a very important part of my healing. They all accepted my disability without making me feel disabled. They did the stretch with me often, and without complaint. They all reached out to help me achieve unrealistic goals that provided a significant quality of life. They may have rolled their eyes more than once but they silently and supportively did the STRETCH along with me. And I am very grateful.

I took a week off to regroup and back to school.

Chapter 16

Devastating

Everything is going well at school that week back. The second week back we were doing a unit on simple and compound machines. A student was working pulleys and he wanted me to help him hold a board while he nailed it to another one. He takes a swing with his hammer and misses and hits the wheelchair and makes this big bang. I went to move and my chair breaks off the bracket from the back of the chair. Now I'm sitting sideways looking down at the floor and the students are screaming for help! The janitor and another teacher arrived and asked what happened? Before I could say anything the student starts crying saying, "I did it when I hit his char with my hammer". The janitor grabbed a chair with wheels and slides me over onto it and wheeled me to my desk. Then I looked up and the student is so upset because he's thinking about what he did. I called him over and told him it's not your fault, the bracket was cracked and that's why it broke. One of the teachers volunteered to take the bracket to have it welded. It took her some time so I had to continue teaching in the office chair. I was slipping down on the chair so the janitor comes in to help me sit better in the chair. He grabs me from the back of the chair and lifts me up and my pants fall down and I don't wear underwear. Now 30 kids are staring at my groin area and I hear one boy say; did you see the size of his balls? I'm asking any student to help us and their response was no way Mr. R. Because the janitor could not pull my pants back up while he was holding me up. I had the class leave until my pants were back on. Boy was I embarrassed. When the class came back in a helper ran around to get my bracket welded and helped me put the chair back together. I'm finally back in my chair and I'm wheeling back into the classroom and it's so quiet you could hear my wheel squeaking from the wax floor. I'm at my desk looking at the kids they're all staring at me waiting for me to say something.

I'm thinking how the hell am I going to handle this, they're all going to tell their parents when they get home. Here goes; kids I want to apologize for what happened earlier today, you have to remember I told you guys that anything can happen in this class and when it does, laugh it off. Everybody think of something funny you did and now let's laugh! We all laugh for a minute and went on with the lesson. That night at home I was waiting for a phone call, but it didn't happen. The next morning I met a parent going into school and I ask her if her daughter told her anything about yesterday's class. Yeah, your chair broke and the whole class felt bad, and you weren't mad about the chair being busted, and you didn't stop your lesson and they had fun while it was broken. I'm saying to myself the kid's didn't say a word about my pants falling.

The bell rings and the class comes in and gets ready for class. My buddy gets up and says; Mr. R. I'm speaking for the class, none of us told their parents about your pants falling off, we know it wasn't your fault, and we didn't want our parents to go bitch to the principal. We know he doesn't like you, we love you Mr. R. I started to cry and thank them all. The rest of the day was great. The weekend was here and Jeanne and I were going shopping at North Conway Saturday. With everything that happened this week I needed a break from being a wheeling hazard. We headed out in the morning and had a great day with Jeanne saw a movie and did a little shopping. I'm driving into Berlin by the Cleveland Bridge, I stop for the red light than it turns green, I take off and the van is making this knocking noise from the transmission and I rolled into an old garage station parking lot and now the van won't go forward. I look at Jeanne and said; hang on we're going home in reverse. We were 3 miles from home. When I started to go in reverse and people were honking their horn.

I pulled up at the intersection on Main Street waiting for the light to go green, Jeanne and I are looking right at the car in front of me, they are telling me I am going backwards and I should turn the van around and go the right way. Dunkin Donuts is right at this intersection and there was a group of people telling me

I'm going the wrong way. The light turns green and I'm off in reverse heading up Pleasant Street than I turn on Hillside to head home and more people were blowing their horn. Now someone stops me and before he could say anything I told him my transmission blew and all I had was reverse and I'm almost home. We finally make it home and Jeanne and I laughed about the faces people were making while I was driving home in reverse.

I'm at home thinking of everything I have to do now because I don't have transportation to school until the transmission gets fixed. The next year was frustrating we were totally computerized which is confusing. It was a lot of work in school and preparation took forever. The science fair didn't get any better, the kids were getting lazy. All subjects were on the computer. My boss always had a new program to use every month. Most of the staff would bitch about it behind his back, I had one teacher say oh he is like my younger brother, of course she did most of his work! Pull your head out of his ass girl. A lot of staff members didn't like me, because the kids and I had fun while learning, we were rule breakers. As the time went on my boss was very pushy with me, sometimes I thought he was belittling me. It was tough teaching with another teacher that thinks she's smarter than other staff members. No matter what I did there was always someone looking to stick a knife in my back? So now there are rumors that a teacher is going to lose their jobs next year due to the low attendance. While this was said he was trying not to look at me. I knew then that it would be me. We get observed every year and it's hard to focus on a lesson when your boss hates you. His kids were moving up to the fifth grade and he did not want me teaching them. Now it's getting closer to February vacation and one morning I was heading out to work it was 15 below zero at my house. I headed down my ramp and my chair stopped dead and my forward motion threw me out of my chair and landed in 14 inches f snow and it was windy. I was laying on my school bag thinking this is not the way I want to die. I finally pushed myself to a side position, my pants slip off my butt while I am trying to move. I can feel the cold my legs are having spasms, I'm crying and yelling for my neighbor. Twenty minutes go by and someone finally realized I had fallen. Thankfully she got out of the car and ran to help me sit up. I'm crying, she ran to my house screaming for Jeanne to come and help get me back in the chair. While she went to get Jeanne a neighbor stopped and helped the girls get me in my wheelchair and back in the house. I sat in front of the gas stove and called in sick. You know I've never been so scared of dying, I've been through a lot but this one was close. I guess God wasn't ready for me. And hell, the devil wasn't ready for me either! Ha! Ha!

Back to school to work. The first of April we are sitting in a meeting and one of the teacher asks when we are going to find out who's losing their job. He looked right at me when he said soon. Its three weeks before spring vacation, Monday 3:30pm. I'm looking out my window and I see the big boss getting out of his vehicle with paper work in his hand. I'm saying here they come I'm going to lose my job. Ten minutes later big boss wants to meet.

They sit down and pull out this folder with a written document backing them up that they get rid of who they want without school board permission. Before they could finish I asked both of them to leave. I didn't need to hear anymore I know what's going on. The big boss says that was easy. I'm thinking what am I going to tell Jeanne. I felt like I committed a crime, the big boss says; don't say anything to the staff. When the door shut I started to cry and cry thinking I am a bad teacher no one is going to hire me and cried even more. My gut was hurting I left my room and told a few more teachers and I had to leave the school before any students saw me. It was the longest ride home, I had to stop I was crying and vomiting out the window. When I finally reached home, I got out and called Jeanne at work. I knew it was going to knock her for a loop. I was crying so hard I couldn't say it, finally it came out. A friend came in the house and grabbed the phone and explained to Jeanne what happened. It was the worst night ever. Jeanne thought I did something wrong at school and I wouldn't tell her. It was easy I did not like the way things changed. In my mind they were changed to satisfy his ego and he did not care who he stepped on. I didn't kiss his ass like everyone else. He didn't like that the kids had a great rapport with me and they did not care for him. For a man with no teaching skills he sure knew a lot about nothing but computers. I had a student punch me he didn't do anything and did not ask him to apologize at all, he didn't report it either because that would make him look bad. I could say more but if you had him for a boss you would know what I'm talking about.

When I went back to school on Tuesday and the teachers are all sorry even the ones that stuck several knifes in my back during my school years. Before the kids came in, I went to see my niece who's a speech therapist at our school. I was telling her that I was so mad that I wanted to kick his ass. Well one of his kiss ass teachers heard me and ran to the boss and tattled on me. I started the day off with the class and had to leave I was crying too much to focus on anything.

I received a phone call around 6:30pm and was told rumor was that I had threatened the boss and was going to beat him up. Can you imagine me doing something to him? If I tried I probably would hurt myself. I wouldn't waste my time trying. I ended up with three weeks off and I was told to come back after spring break. Jeanne and I fought about this whole situation for several weeks. Spring vacation was done and back to work on Monday. He was coming in checking on me seeing if I was doing my job. Asking student's what's going on in this class. By Thursday he had brought my blood pressure up, my sugar was out of whack. He was being an ass and he came in my room and said "do you want the rest of the year of with pay"? I agreed and left. I said bye to the staff member crying my ass off while the kids were saying bye to me at each class, I felt like a loser.

They had the science fair which sucked according to the kids. I wanted to go to graduation but I would have cried the whole time. You know, I loved all those kids and made a difference for several of them. All these hard years of making sure my kids have fun while learning. I met a lot of great parents and some not so great. You can't please everybody.

I'm in my van driving to the unemployment office to start collecting for 26 weeks until my social security is effective. Boy what a pain in the ass it was to get that over with. Retirement isn't bad, a lot of hunting time and more time with Jeanne. I do the laundry, set the table, get supper ready and wait for her to come home so I can tell her about my day and listen to hers.

I know I'm still not settled. I still want to go further. The other day we had a camp sponsored by Polaris Corporation. I started to wheel down where the festival was and I began to slide and I stopped and said; I'm not going any further before something happens. There are chairs with tracks that would have given me a chance to check all the merchants without breaking my electric chair, but too expensive to buy. I'm still going to find ways to do things to help me make a better life for me and my family. No matter how many times I fail or something happens to me, I will laugh it off and move forward. Life's too short to complain about it. I thought I was done but the other day it was nice out, I decided to have a small fire in my man made fireplace, in my backyard. The fire was going well until the wind picks up and blew some hot ashes on the ground that had dry leaves. A grass fire started and I grabbed a hose went back to the fire and my rear tires sunk in the ground and the hose wrapped around the front tires. I couldn't move and the fire is coming right at me, it was two feet away. The trees are on fire and the wind is blowing hard, I had to fall out of my chair and drag myself to the front of the house to get some help. When I was dragging myself across the grass my pants fell off and now I'm bare assed again laying across the driveway like a dead deer that got hit by a car. My neighbor heard my screaming and called 911 then she came over and pulled my pants up till the fire department showed up. She did tell me I had a nice butt. Within minutes they put the fire out and put me back in my chair. Fireman told me no more fires in the backyard unless you have supervision.

Why Did I Write This Book?

I had to reflect and confirm that my life didn't stop after my accident, I knew I had limits with my disability but with the support I had from my family and friends I wanted to exceed those limits. I wanted Jeanne, Jessica, Nathan and my family to be proud of their dad because in my mind I felt like I failed them when I had my accident and I didn't want to fail them again. I never stopped setting goals. There were many obstacles. I want people to know that my life didn't stop because of my accident. The drive inside of me comes from my wife Jeanne, those dark eyes and her look gives me the courage to go forward and not look back. Because that was yesterday and today is a new day. I question God a lot, he never answers me verbally, but I know he's there to help guide my way.

him from the wheelchair to the Jeep Wrangler to take him out for rides to get him out of the house. Little did I know at the time that someday he would be driving me around in his "buggy" showing me such beautiful places in the "Great North Woods" (our backyard) I never, ever, thought that would ever be possible. I'm so happy to admit that I was so, so wrong.

Throughout all the ups, downs, accidents, and all those, "little things that matter" that we take for granted, I have never heard Norman or Jeanne ever complain about anything. Life goes on and every day is a new adventure.

I feel so fortunate and lucky to have been friends with these two wonderful individuals for nearly four decades, when we get together, it's all about enjoying each other's company and laughter. They balance each other so well. They're supposed to be together. They are truly a special couple.

Lucille